Mako Sharks

by Nico Barnes

WITHDRAWN

ABDO
SHARKS
Kids

www.abdopublishing.com

Published by Abdo Kids, a division of ABDO, PO Box 398166, Minneapolis, Minnesota 55439.

Copyright © 2015 by Abdo Consulting Group, Inc. International copyrights reserved in all countries. No part of this book may be reproduced in any form without written permission from the publisher.

Printed in the United States of America, North Mankato, Minnesota.

052014

092014

 THIS BOOK CONTAINS RECYCLED MATERIALS

Photo Credits: Corbis, Getty Images, Glow Images, Minden Pictures, Science Source, Thinkstock

Production Contributors: Teddy Borth, Jennie Forsberg, Grace Hansen

Design Contributors: Candice Keimig, Laura Rask, Dorothy Toth

Library of Congress Control Number: 2013952577

Cataloging-in-Publication Data

Barnes, Nico.

 Mako sharks / Nico Barnes.

   p. cm. -- (Sharks)

ISBN 978-1-62970-067-0 (lib. bdg.)

Includes bibliographical references and index.

1. Mako sharks--Juvenile literature.   I. Title.

597.3--dc23

                          2013952577

Table of Contents

Mako Sharks

Mako sharks live in oceans around the world. They are usually found near the water's **surface**.

4

Some makos live close
to shores. Others live
far out at sea.

Makos have large, black eyes.

They have long, pointed noses.

9

Makos are small sharks.

But they are strong.

11

Makos are built for speed. They are one of the fastest sharks.

Hunting

Makos have long, skinny teeth.

They are perfect for biting **prey**.

15

Mako sharks hunt down their **prey**. They bite their prey and swallow them whole.

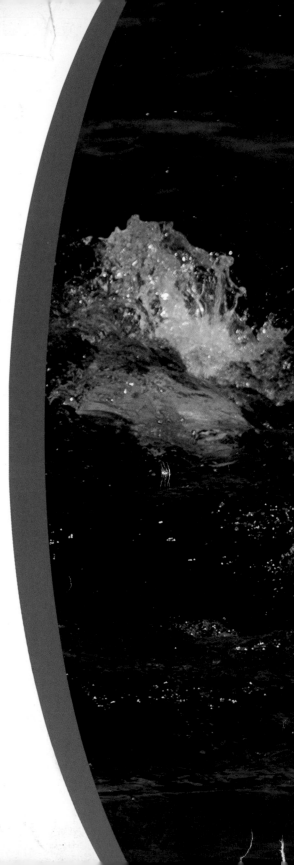

Food

Makos eat many types
of fish. They sometimes
eat squid and sea turtles.

Baby Mako Sharks

Baby mako sharks are called **pups**. Mothers give birth to 4 to 16 pups at a time. Pups swim away from their mothers after birth.

More Facts

- Mako sharks are known for jumping very high out of the water. They can jump more than 20 feet (6 m).

- Mako sharks are one of the smartest sharks.

- If a fisherman catches a swordfish, there is a good chance you will find a mako shark nearby. Mako sharks like to eat swordfish, and they both like the same **environments**.

Glossary

environment – everything that surrounds and affects a living thing.

prey – an animal hunted or killed for food.

pup – a newborn animal.

surface – the top of a body of water.

Index

abdokids.com

Use this code to log on to abdokids.com and access crafts, games, videos and more!

Abdo Kids Code:
SMK0670